Inspecting Nostalgia

INSPECTING NOSTALGIA

R. Kolewe

Talonbooks

© 2017 Ralph Kolewe

All rights reserved. No part of this book may be reproduced, stored in a retrieval system, or transmitted, in any form or by any means, without the prior written consent of the publisher or a licence from Access Copyright (The Canadian Copyright Licensing Agency). For a copyright licence, visit accesscopyright.ca or call toll free to 1-800-893-5777.

Talonbooks
278 East First Avenue, Vancouver, British Columbia, Canada V5T 1A6
www.talonbooks.com

First printing: 2017

Typeset in Garamond
Printed and bound in Canada on 100% post-consumer recycled paper

Interior design by Chloë Filson
Cover design by Typesmith
Cover painting: "Roses" (1878) by George Cochran Lambdin (1830–1896), published by L. Prang & Co. Courtesy the Boston Public Library

Talonbooks gratefully acknowledges the financial support of the Canada Council for the Arts, the Government of Canada through the Canada Book Fund, and the Province of British Columbia through the British Columbia Arts Council and the Book Publishing Tax Credit.

Library and Archives Canada Cataloguing in Publication

Kolewe, R. (Ralph), 1957–, author

    Inspecting nostalgia / poems by R. Kolewe.

ISBN 978-1-77201-132-6 (softcover)

    I. Title.

PS8621.O47I57 2017   C811'.6   C2017-900721-1

"You can't say it that way any more."

—*John Ashbery*

"Pleasure is stubborn, in retrospect, with nowhere to end."

—*Lyn Hejinian*

Contents

The fixed stars — 1
    Before — 3
    Temporal — 4
    Given — 6
    In a winter field — 8
    A smooth envelope — 9
    "Time is lyric's dark counterpoise." — 11
    A clock in the shape of — 13
    The fixed stars — 15
    Lawn chairs — 16
    The result is not simple — 17

Suppressed details — 19
    "To understand a proposition means to know what is the case if it is true." — 21
    Packing up — 23
    Five common praises (not divine) — 24
    Five cuttings — 25
    Overpainted photographs — 26
    Lyric interlude: from an abandoned essay — 28
    Triangle — 29
    Some contents — 30
    The clear, clean room — 31

Vanishing lessons	33
Vanishing lesson	35
"She didn't learn to tell time until her mid-teens"	36
Hearing the western wind	37
They were expecting a description	38
With dark centres	39
How their voices	40
Where the resemblance is most striking	41
"In the rain, as if there were no need for a taxi to take us away"	42
To find what is found wanting in a crowd (1)	43
The divergence between enjoying and knowing	44
To find what is found wanting in a crowd (2)	45
Is it courtship if it's on paper like flowers	46
To find what is found wanting in a crowd (3)	47
Under	48
Learning the risk of colour at night	49
Marginal notes from an essay on desire	51
The truth in painting	83
Is this hidden away	85
Critique of the power of aesthetic judgment	86
A taxonomy, an anatomy	87
They go on in the same discourse	88
Necessary litany	90
Add to this	91
Instead of resolving the problem	92
The light that leaks from composition	93
If I am compelled	94
Materials	95
The original of	96
If I am completely calm	97

An excess	98
Life. Or, still life.	99
Erased	100
Doubt comes before belief	101
And innumerable times again	102
I thought I knew	103
Leaving or arriving	104
Perhaps touching	105
To find the real	106
How much past to set aside	107
The truth in painting	108
Beyond measure	109
Not after	110
Memory frame	111
Inspecting nostalgia	**113**
Afterword and critique	123
Sources	**127**
Acknowledgments	**131**

The fixed stars

Before

Bringing home flowers
driving past the fire hall
it was all imaginary roses
it was all imaginary music
and the bees circling
round that sweetness
were almost singing.
Could such beauty
go unremarked?
I think not. I think
I still say your name
repeatedly
and it will not become
imaginary. I think the fire
will not go out for lack
of singing. I think the real
of every rose
is that conflagration:
those petals, your name.

Temporal

I want to ask you then
true grace against false beginning
like rain the simplest last night's

message all over again.
Intermittency.
The memory of a joy is not joyous

or flame or open, I know.
It moves from hand to hand, mine, yours
like a pencil

as you drew
your enthusiastic independent ecstasy,
lines I couldn't follow.

Ask how after all this I can want
and I do, toward the above
of the future which is pure quiet

which I am not yet.
Your name beginning and ending now
voluntary not a word of time or weather.

The choice to forget perhaps
knowing that I have forgotten, knowing
this is not called upon to be sincere.

Given

There was rearrangement looking back,
green stems and yellow stars on black,
daffodils in the tea bowl, bulbs barely buried.

Can I honestly say there was nothing hidden there?
Maybe nothing happened, neither
reassurance nor oppression, or if so

only cleared plates after the plain kitchen's
pale-blue flame, its slack
lamentation and the dust-grey tabby

scratching at your stepsister's window,
the morning paper of frost before spring.
There was a small tear in the shoulder

of your dress, a green wool dress
I never saw you wear, bought
for the occasion of this memory.

Your stocking feet propped up
on the empty adjacent wicker seat
beside a cabinet of familiar landscapes

or landscape paintings, retouched. A waterfall.
You were reading and only paused once,
turning a page, but said nothing.

In a winter field

The beauty of certain animals say a horse.
Say a horse in a winter field in late afternoon black-and-white
almost untouched by snow.
Reading this you can imagine I've described.
A minor key light and solitude with a meaning.
You can imagine a strength or inquiry.

Standing at the wire
fence without gloves and numb in the wind
almost untouched by snow
without an apple or sugar or lyric thought
across the late afternoon black-and-white
in the other corner of a winter field.

If I repeat myself you can imagine a solitude or a description
or the wind in the stiff remaining stubble or a lyric thought.
If I repeat myself the beauty of certain animals regardless.

A smooth envelope

Perfect or imperfect, prolonged or entirely enclosed
by the past I believe you knowing how difficult it is to lie
or even just read aloud in a simple uninflected voice.

There was a river. There was an island, a tower. A bridge.
There, this morning is the colour of those envelopes.
It is spring, there is snow on the high

angled roofs so I think of them as roofs again.
How light the paper. Not really blue,
but shades of violet, mauve, lavender

and purple, violet-purple, bluish-purple
sometimes the purple bruised and sometimes a promise,
a sunset after thunder, wet pigment, a veil, a tissue –

usually a smooth envelope, pale sky *par avion*,
even though I almost never wrote them.
I am always saying this to you. By now the ice has broken

away. I feel this winter slipping away.
Whatever is nearest opened the windows.
How many versions? I will fold this over,

turn it back like the plain white sheet on my bed.
There are gulls and the beginning of clouds,
the dried grasses confused at the river's edge.

Snowmelt. Sunlight's straight edges
on cotton, paper, now open water. Address written out
in lovely blueness, enclosed, prolonged, printed last.

> "Time is lyric's dark counterpoise."
>
> —*Jan Zwicky*

Tomorrow barely begins to breathe,
is impossible to remember at the end
of after in a season of parting. Perhaps
that's too much and why sequence appeals.
Breathing now is simple and takes no time.

Holding everything back until
but it isn't then. Foreclosed.
Tomorrow spreads like a tree in leaf.
Time lapses. In another forest your
path is too deep in leaving.

Only now and memory acts entirely in the present.
Is this confusing? Means coming together means
in which the distinction of the elements
is lost by blending or intimate intermingling
but also discomfiture, overthrow, ruin, perdition.

Because boundaries are comfortable
and time overthrows them.
I thought leaves falling information
the angles of remembering and recall
like gravity. Want being what isn't now.

That's always past if
I had done this then read
with just the right voice, tone,
and breathing
between now and now an infinity of sharp points

repeating returns
between you and you and I and I another
series that crosses out time. You were always
impatient when I said there's no time
for that or other things I loved. Still.

A clock in the shape of

a heart she said and always
she said. Is there listening in that?
I don't know I can listen to you.

It's a kind of astronomy. I always go back
there, the constellations, lines drawn
on top of it, the tick of it,

the just get it down of it and where
does it end. It doesn't, that's
a trick. Spaced at intervals, taken

as it comes, it came, that time
was all about running out of time
wasn't it, you tell me I'm not listening

to my anger maybe that's ticking, talking –
listen we hadn't figured it out yet
those days, I hadn't, maybe

you did. You always told me
I listened instead of being there.
But the constellations were your idea.

It's a kind of astronomy, not accuracy, you said.
We lay there, listening. A clock
was ticking, and you know we still want

clocks to tick I think this idea
of the heart is also a kind of constellation.
I can't conclude but I always go back.

I want to listen, not talk. That's true
at least as true as that time
and that time I didn't know what I was hearing

that I was hearing astronomy
unaware of revolution or anger or anything
but you beside me looking up

specifically at Orion you pointed
I put that star there you said
it fell later in many ways true.

The fixed stars

1

My dear star, star I held in my cold hand just once, that
 opened and started, bloomed and dried, cool bright moth –

Star tree curled up into nights and days, sprouting all the
 constellations, leaves in milk-clear sky that fall

and fell out of my hand. Exactly entirely distant burning like a
 letter. New light you said. Always falling in straight lines.

2

I have never climbed an apple tree
mistaking a dark unfallen unpicked apple
against the night for the fresh, eclipsed moon.

3

Every star whose name you never learned written out in full,
 looped and lettered and left in the new cool dark, the night
 a tree full of bright and me climbing in it, not knowing
 you at all.

Lawn chairs

At that time stars were brighter.
There were more of them.
We sat outside on aluminum
lawn chairs with green and white plastic

star webbing, watched satellites
and meteors. I
pointed them out said look.
Sometimes wasn't believed

but I had all the answers except later no story
to make it all fall out differently.

Under dark windows wishing they would fill with stars.
The kind of cheap light lawn chair everybody had.

That's it.

The result is not simple

The rain woke me I wanted it to be
you, could hear your voice or footsteps
or memory. 5:15 a.m. For a long time
I got up early, time being only
adds to itself, entropy, geometry, margin,
or the book at my bedside and
always leaving the window open.
In alphabetical order.
Careless desolation simply.
I should turn back to tell it right
repeating and not repeating astonishment.

Suppressed details

> "To understand a proposition means to know what is the case if it is true."
>
> —*Tractatus* 4.024

1

Falling past the imagine
Falling past the limbic beautiful
Falling past the skeletal rider

Falling past the tautology nerve
Falling past the past
Falling past the pure aesthetic direction proposal

Falling past the new activity on
Falling past the repeat modulation of memory consolidation
Falling past the angel and the serotonin orchid, almond, feather, planet, dance, seize, lift –

2

The draft, the attempt, the etched plate un-inked with shadow un-blacked un-dyed un- or the passage of or the blood of or an audience or a conscript or a participant or an inside or a necessary MRI. No one is necessary. No one is inside. There is no inside, no dove-grey false colour. Farther.

3

Falling light rain wind centromedial in rats and cats
from the northeast and mist curve bias
almost calm the drizzle hardly.

Sunrise at 7:52 a.m.
Every day a bit off if embodied.
Outside there is no outside.

A thin edge, a between sustained enhancements of signalling.
A pale-white dawn I.
Unwarranted winter memories associated with emotional
    events.

Packing up

We could try again. Of course not.
Narrow white doors leaning up against the white porch
like moonbeams. It's called a crescent wrench.

Warm light machine oil on our fingers.
Scent and slip.
Oiled stainless vernier calipers precise to a thousandth of
    an inch

in a dark oiled rectangular wood box. The top slides off.
A dark crescent indent. Being proud
we have no use for them.

We have them. We could try again.
Measure. Precise ghost light from our neighbour's neighbour's
dwelling. More boxes on the porch.

Books, instructions, pictures, stories that have endings.

Five common praises (not divine)

My compassion is delimited or repeated this.

A *taut* line over the *narrow* sky and your *bright* skirts *quick* drying.

Every alley surrenders into [a] vocabulary.

Follow we sing *stumbling*. I suppress detail.

Say your name (only your name) once in another city.

Five cuttings

At some time order gave way and I lost count of scissors, scraps, anaesthesia, other etc.

Suture bright red heart red invisible red drawn through flesh my affect. Or is that.

Skin cloth rolled and fastened with shark teeth, rolled and stored in a card box with bone, theology, air, if moonlight I will refuse food. I will refuse.

Can I say what I. Never said listen. Never said look. Not beautiful or now feeling.

I don't want decision healing your name, needles, or knives. Don't talk back to me. Who –

(often vengeance, one plant divided and divided and divided immortal cut again, impure cut, blessed, infected, unsealed, unsaid, bled)

Overpainted photographs

I had hoped for more.

I had hoped for calculus, or image, or oracle.

I had hoped for definition.

I had hoped for more than market forces, for science which is not certainty but.

I had hoped for.

I had hoped for mathematics at least hope.

I had hoped for the surface of equations.

I had hoped for economy or psychology.

I had hoped for an algebra at least.

I had hoped for more than tickets weighted down so the wind.

I had hoped for more than irony or ceremony.

I had hoped for income streams.

I had hoped for plate tectonics more topical the Higgs boson a pandemic.

I had hoped for the waitress (Lindsay) to acknowledge that I'd noticed that she had dyed her hair.

I had hoped for illness, that I'd be done by now.

I had hoped for flowers gladioli at the shop on the corner they looked like they'd been left out in the frost.

I had hoped turning would be as good as being reborn.

I had hoped a handful of pharmaceuticals at bedtime would be a continent, a galaxy, a red shift, a light cone, a Lockheed Model 10 Electra that would say enough.

I had hoped without remembering because memory.

I had hoped for memory to hang behind.

I had hoped for memory to last familiar as Maillol's sculpture, always the same woman.

I had hoped for enough like the wind functional or opening or chalk on board or ink or pencil-crayon scratch continue I had hoped for continue as it does in Plato even though my handwriting is hard to read without maps and algebra again a clear view of the sky to five satellites wait they will acquire.

I had hoped for did I write to you that I was early but I always am so I thought of a small game my hand resting a curtain or a simple Poisson distribution or the words that are not exchanged with the prince a communion.

I had hoped for aporia but nothing you could call history now or recollected trajectory.

I had hoped for nothing but corners and stars freed from constellations and planets and prosody. A standard text. Egyptian cotton. Blankets. Painting.

Lyric interlude: from an abandoned essay

I'm part-sick of every paring.
Ask, could this life be ever sharper?

Hold wire, hold creased thought, myelin white. Only paper.
Ask, is there another lifted, another fertile response?

Your vivacity is my rushing in.
Ask, what are you afraid of?

Nothing keeps me here or you.
Not the seduction of yield or ending.
Not listening to names. Not answering city.

I stay. The impossible after subject now.
Want to haunt the pleasure of photons and notation.
Want to stop ask colour anyone.

Triangle

1

Making something beautiful isn't always.
The cage is locked. The key
isn't knowing. I don't know what the key is.

2

There are three sides to every history I've found
myself looking back at points A and B
seeing and wondering and desire.

3

I hold an empty glass dream.
We take our obsessions Bacon said and we pour them in.
We don't choose them but want them know I do.

4

Let me bring you sweet drizzled with indigo
bruised or robes or innocent with honey
twilight growth in the shadow of my hands.

Some contents

1.1 Allure.
1.2 Thirty-one full-colour plates.
1.3 Avoiding hereditary disease.
1.4 Contingent, inward, antecedent, nearest.

2.1 Each thought significant perturbation.
2.2 Purity famine of the abstract open.
2.3 A differentiable bijection is not necessarily a diffeomorphism.
2.4 Counter-transference.

3.1 The morbid anatomy of the premature subject.
3.2 Pellucid marginal degeneration.
3.3 Recursions can be easily transformed to iterations.
3.4 *Diamonds are a girl's best friend.*

4.1 Parentheses, interruption, deference, semicolon.
4.2 The number isn't in the book.

The clear, clean room

The professionals start from a different place.
Not systematically, but randomly.
They get lost.
This is what isn't poetry supposed to be
finding your authentic voice.
The photograph is silent, a barking dog.
It's a totally human conclusion.
The clear, clean room and the outside world
projected upside down, a bit dim, quiet
on the cracked plaster wall of the attic
half the lath torn off. See the nails. Why did they do that?
And how do you remove yourself from the poem?
During the second, remedial session, I use Polaroid Type 665
Positive/Negative film and shoot until the subject is happy.

Vanishing lessons

Vanishing lesson

A black bird, the smell of gone oranges
and grey as gentle rain spread like ink
at disappearing. Try it. Look.

Colouring out all movement
I'm even better than you at this
here. Wrapped in ghost seasons,

looking first looking back,
sit and see and fill with clouds
stopped by a wet storm-grey-green park bench.

That skirt, you say, has a life of its own.
You have a life of your own.
Your shadow winters me with vanishing.

"She didn't learn to tell time until her mid-teens"

Say now.
Say pure motion might be
time's desire left in us to move.

Say moving.
Say want no matter
what scan of chance returns.

Say moved.
Say more but never simply.
Being never less dangerous than repeated.

Hearing the western wind

How years are not held they pass
and circumstance yet
in attachment blossoms fall and in aversion

it rains, it rains, a small rain
that doesn't shake the trees
the street lamp passing for the moon

in broken puddles
to make a list of things (walls or beds)
you may abandon if you wish.

They were expecting a description

The word "caress," or careless or satchel or, if need be, a fortune teller, a notebook, a square, or the postponed task of washing the floor, or menu or carnival or body shop or because, fascinating, foundering, hooded, private, a school bus, to take down a notch. Carbon.

The clear table.
The quiet morning.
The blank screen.
The unmarked page.

The new house.
The calm mind.
The open hours.
The minimum.

How do I say that, and what does it mean?
Breathing frequency.
Atlas. Anterior or interior or flirtation.

How does wonder, which is a kind of error, swerve?
When the wind comes from the northwest, more or less, and there is rain, heavy, leakage occurs.
I have not understood a thing, revise.

With dark centres

Waking everything is ordinary not forgetting.
A slice of sun edging the tabletop, a bowl of milk
on the rough woven red place-cloth
revised
to continuous shadow, to painting, to printing, to the young frame
the beautiful, the litany, the repeating, the red having

become mauve daybreak. The lyric ended
yesterday again, and, see, I'm falling
backwards now. Did that happen to you or only written –

You and there are. Flowers in a blush
on the table, big blown poppies, or
perhaps they're tulips after all, matter,

red, red, red, with dark centres.
Morning cools. It can't still be spring.

How their voices

Lying in the cold under
all-frayed aurora and the brief stars
that I imagined everything

everyone knows rough edges and listening
in twilight in the woods in the fresh snow
unwrapping, embassy, folly, arrow, method, plan:

glimpse of thin high cloud peaceful true orphanage
like colour photographs torn out
of the *New Yorker*. The next day overcast, four degrees.

Where the resemblance is most striking

I like to peel oranges so
the peel becomes a long bitter spiral, one piece
that can curl up to simulate
an orange again.

A few years ago someone I assume young wove
blue, white, and orange plastic strapping
through the chain-link fence around the tennis court
in the park spelling out words. It was snowing

when I first saw them. They weren't words
immediately. Later there was a picture on the Internet.

"In the rain, as if there were no need for a taxi to take us away"

Like another yet to see
I took a photograph of you
in the taxi mirror mimicking a different life on Lexington
 knowing
 not knowing but wanting more than wanting reflection
I stumbled on the curb
emptying everything into the large of the rain.

In the hidden opening in the broken lines in the
I will not remember for you
retreat to street signs
no entry yield one way maximum etc. the walking man on fire
 with frail gesture again.
They are recognized everywhere I am.

To find what is found wanting
in a crowd (1)

No conversation, can't say could you
pass me that. So keep things
in reach, or don't make the effort.

I read the same books again and again.
My understanding is corrupt.
I want fragments, shards. I want desire.

I think of myself that's inaccurate.
Where I am, _____ is. A crowd
of outline I breathe through the gaps.

The divergence between enjoying and knowing

You can keep looking I can
look closer step back
this is a detail time
affected pleasurably by
the image of a thing past or future
but there is only one first.

Grey-green sage-green pleasure
that is wormwood aromatic
unrelated poppies red black irradiated
colour isn't simple
intimacy is rewritten as it is retrieved.
I will think of you in my other poems.

To find what is found wanting in a crowd (2)

I don't feel threatened by this.
I read the same.
In a garden a crowd given flaws.

Nothing special real gesture.
I don't feel threatened by this.
Water dripping into black soil.

A body thing, a breathing and repeating
gaps until you know because you don't
know you. For now, in a heap, in a pile.

Is it courtship if it's on paper like flowers

Feeling isn't allegory.
Falling isn't direction.
I'm afraid, and I'm not afraid.

Silence is not platonic anyway
there is no silence
varied levels of attention

of you intent at the mirror with lipstick catching my eye
there is a photograph.
No, we can't, can we?

Fall and scatter, shudder, bodies remembered, confused
in error, forgetting only.
Sunshine on cedar. Stairs. Books. Almost noon.

To find what is found wanting
   in a crowd (3)

I think the wraithing time came later.
I want to tell but don't have a tradition.
I so much enjoyed the autumn streets.

The wind and all the window fire.
Seeing through, seeing through. No empty houses.
I'm not threatened by this I read.

In passing in time in conversation outside.
Sorting by myself. Reaching. Not a cause.
A repetition, a gap like breathing.

Under

Now
leap from the sovereign.
Swim in the dark

without direction
eyes closed.
The hiding place always

found out find
a different place to begin
offshore, back up, say.

Words that can only be
uttered in a certain
way, without breathing.

Learning the risk of colour at night

would have to be fences or windows, an upended
boat. Write my grave will be a red tent
like an explanation of grief always comes.

Certainty turns us into phantoms.
Come sleep, the fox, sand-coloured
to distract me, unfinished quotation.

Marginal notes from an essay on desire

1

Loss balanced against present pleasure.
Abandoned meaning.
It was a line thrown. The sea.

A deleted line. Allegorical.
Can't drown in that, unreached.
There is always a thing unsaid.

So say it! I'm asking now
speaking of others. To celebrate,
swim all day, eyes closed, lungs full.

2

Look you. It looms,
it rejects, it is. Mirrored,
it peaks over the waves.

Interrupt silence with event.
The monotony of the diary.
Annapurna is the deadliest mountain on earth.

The phone isn't ringing. Like furies.
Concierge looking, desire
without named territory or self.

3

A euphoric counterpoint the demand.
Of course the gap.
Your note unsatisfied, marginal.

With that I have to stop.
I would arrange things otherwise.
The blue there, the green-white.

All kinds. Underlined.
Reality explains. The leaden
nets written around the bed.

4

Dear, there are cloud
prints on your glass doors.
It's tonic. It's blue. You

make nothing happen.
You deliver eve. You swallow.
You loop again. You loop again.

Test the beginning or the end.
I can't dive or give birth to waves.
Clarity is desire clarity.

5

The whole world starts to.
All of it at a distance.
An echo. A round fog idea. A bell.

All about another day.
I listened to a sound I don't know how to make.
Game. Recollecting

that is to say putting back
together what has been broken
into space, into play, into music.

6

Scratch down and then spill, a point
or a direction, a night or ten,
a curl of ink, a rose, a re-enactment –

Tear this out. This is my trivial world.
Un-staged. I dream that way.
Cello loops. Air ropes. Blood knots. Fuel.

You're on your own word by word
from that scratch. One begin, one high fire.
A picture of the end of the world, circa 1965.

7

A picture of the end, the world, today, neither.
A bearded man sitting with a painted cup of steam erased
in this wordless drowning rain. All rust. No listening.

All shall be. How optimism annihilates.
And all shall be. How reassurance undermines.
Mama, I need a muse to rescue me today.

That ambulance don't stop here anymore.
The audience has migrated into all I
don't understand this defeat of art and feeling.

8

Regret or recognition. Black earth of past lives.
The yellow leaves ending this year.
The pale paper beets in the salad.

Not here can't vanish I said but it's not true.
Hope fucks it up, a warm October day.
After the salad, *boeuf bourguignon*. Is that red? Sure is.

What I've lost waiting for these black letters to arrive.
Those I sent, and those I only hope were sent to me.
Then dessert, an idea of colour darkening into sunset.

9

A slice of someone else's. Orange, she said. Too full. Full stop.
The passionate knot, the moment. Decisive, she can't decide.
If I tell you nothing, she said, will you keep.

Well here I am. Still or is it again still.
Halfway through some kind. Expect clearing.
The start of the I began. The woods have changed now.

There's a sad man like this in every bar beauty,
truth, strangeness, and charm, unframed prints.
Something sublime is supposed to happen now.

10

Control any PC remotely.
Self-publish a book.
A hundred-year moratorium,

performed in cemeteries
replies upon, but cannot own,
and then flowers as if –

oxford grammar art matter
tasty boys and girls cartel suburbs
typical one half-stop f-number scale

11

Obsession is like that. Rust.
Today is like that. Cut.
I don't need presence to make a list.

Numbers what I come back to. Laugh.
The parking lot across from you. Books.
The word for when clocks counted.

Is it voicemail now press star.
Is it fire and appliance colony.
Is it renamed or solitary.

12

Only edges now, no verbs, holes cut out
of the page where actions were. Resplendent anarchy.
If I could remember I would be touched again.

What do I know about that now?
My working notes have been drowned in tap water.
An impossible description of that unknown

theorems cloud. Erased into visibility.
Refusing to be addressed. Rendered
as a postponed abstract not embodied. All wrong.

13

Hearing the refrigerator. Less or at least.
Why does love? Slip. Translate.
One in thirty wearing grief and noise.

Well it's a good way to go. Or.
The abandon isn't exactly alphabetic.
Lots of empty now. Of sequence. Lots exactly.

Loud safe affections. Is that of time
the conversation what we're left with, heartbreak
and oak groves, Dufferin laurel Bloor.

14

Objects survive. The world does not.
A rainbow watch. A thin watch.
A dead man's watch keeps on, green.

Let me repeat this I can I am
not the man I used to be
yet I undertake to. Unquote.

This is my horizon this gate
made manifest. Abandoned like hope
and collected and dusted once in a while, by others.

15

Evolution without streets
drawing not things seen
no echoes no fact not time then.

Real disparity exists
a loom a scarf a tension
multi-cored and threaded.

Mine in my stomach confirmed
another triad of past
my address epic and novel now.

16

A bracelet of Novembers, carnelian
nights without snow and twisting roads.
There was a door opening. An old novel.

The sky is knotted with laurel
and telephone numbers. Listen.
If I could answer Petrarch I wouldn't need.

It's a private eye tough guy gin
mill kind of letter, left under
the door when you weren't watching. Okay?

17

I need to look more keenly at childish things.
I need at least 116 reasons for.
I need the consolation of conceal and be plain.

I need the stone thrown into my reflection.
I need this long goodbye, this too-accurate list.
I need the real word scar after the mirror.

I need a postcard and shards of knife-black type.
I need the book of Revelation.
I need the lyric turn, another turn, your turn now.

18

This is not matter. The day I conceived
essence and several species of scraps
another said I felt and now and now & now.

This is clear. I'm missing something.
Cold me in the broken hard outside.
Is it hailing another said it's hailing.

Look you. Another's own narrative. Look.
This is where I go beyond empty rescue.
This is where I stop translation.

19

The torn gilt cloth that covers us is not
won by any will, always grace, always
another dancer, sovereign but legitimately

desired (but all desire is) – does it precede
invitation and idiom, just plain
broken prose that my tongue cuts itself

on, its sharp flowers seducing us both, yes, again,
after too many gifts and deaths, too many little
confessions to the perfect future? Tell me. You.

20

This requires will beyond furnace white to see.
Your life goes untouched by. Now you
and how many others stand tigers

in your bright quiet kitchens taking dishes off
the table, salt, completely ordinary life
and theatre. And then? You were completely ordinary

then, I was. Well beyond that plain quick symmetry I slept,
got up in the morning un-confused. Not innocence,
not experience, this glowing disquiet, our time and art.

21

This is hinged.
This is torn.
This means change. The subject now.

Late under the night's perfection
circling the beautiful north left alley
a black sand mood in PowerPoint. Circumspect.

It wants to ring again.
That is almost turned up half.
Alarming silence.

22

If I made something
sublime a door would open
you would open it.

I papered the walls with sky.
I thought I could not ask you.
The wind blew, the wind blew.

You left in the owl-haunted dawn.
Dreamt white wings, electricity.
Then your grey eyes, storm clouds, sleep.

23

I long to visit by the word,
can't tell what my eyes are like,
how my hands feel action at a distance.

Learn all about arguments near you it says here.
Old rumours have it that I gave it all away.
Never wrote a letter, not once night fell.

You were blind for days, hoping
I had never seen a mirror broken that way.
You never think of it now. I'm sure.

24

A hemming-in. A finished edge
when I want tatters and trod upon.
Like tearing pages out of books

and throwing them into the ocean
in the wake of your crossing.
How does that go? Yes or no?

Recite the speech again. No audience.
"A hemming-in. A finished edge
when I want tatters and trod upon."

25

A keen or prescient ability to speak
constantly on this subject. My own ghost.
Meaning I don't exist can't effect

anything. Exactly how is that beginning
different than a real story? Tell.
These nights go on too long to dark.

Inspection fills them but with
the end-over-end of past
and past, and better, past. Now.

26

How often can this permanent.
This strategy or memory if.
This wire or garden love if.

This all-over crossing if.
This azure O! calendar if.
This high apple core if.

How much does obsession scatter.
It's too quiet. Too almost. Too sandy.
This simultaneous lifetime now.

27

I haven't looked back. I'm not
convinced. That's not my story.
I could say it all. Wrong the same or later.

Stairs and a subway gate. A bargain
serpent destination holiday crossed off.
Tree pool. Spring street. River roof.

At last I need a striking image here.
Like an asp. The idea of stain.
Emptying light remains. Not torn at all.

The truth in painting

Is this hidden away

your brush with words pure
disinterested delight
coming later, later then
not at all now
knowing
this beautiful beyond pleasure certainly
but also
order never mattered
and

a picture of that tree again.

Critique of the power of aesthetic judgment

These trees are not an orchard
not a forest or
economy, alone, household, archaic

not seen a way
to avoid speech and understanding
shadows drystone wall

clear sound through empty branches
catching pendant
spring before leaves but now definitely gone.

There is no science of the beautiful.

A taxonomy, an anatomy

No leaves yet the tree stripped into tangle ribbed back
inside saying nothing in the senses
solitary, averse in whatever dictionary remains to me

emphasizes differences stationary monochrome.
Dusk. That soft name not resolve or refuge, mute.
Leaving? A body? Trait? Shadow? Pitch or echo?

The limit, even that of colour.
Not metaphor the forgetfulness which is our complicity
so often around me branch and strength a great fall

of spirit copied, split.

They go on in the same discourse

What is one time, this right time?

It isn't because we remember anymore.

I'm trying to remember when that was, what year –

I don't remember being happy but I still, not nostalgia that's wrong –

Say a leap year came between, say –

I do remember having breakfast in your garden.

You could work out the day of the week it was I think Tuesday but I'm not sure but I could work it out.

The bees!

Or look it up. I used to circle the slow and normal words in the dictionary. You know that?

And there were so many flowers:
cosmos echinacea marguerite gladioli aster yarrow sage phlox monarda –

In Greek κοσμος means ornament and order, regulator, means here & now, also of stars, means extraordinary if –

You make shit up.

I make shit up.

Was that you hurrying alone yesterday?

I think not. A stranger or a cloud maybe.

No need to look back to lose you.

Both of us keep cut flowers far too long.

I said that.

What is it Saint Augustine said about time?

That time I cried.

Do you remember?

Necessary litany

Things draw us not precisely.
Wide glass jars, brushes bent in water and watercolour.
Porcelain, stainless, paper. More.

Breathing wet cedar light ruled out broken on the floor behind
and the cat sleeping on the table as I. Or you.
Thrush. Thick blue. Line and sky. Evening.

After abandon becomes giving some
of my books still alphabetized.
Halfway in our always forest necessary.

Thanks to everyone who said keep on writing these things.
Outside history quiet wings.
Perfection has often been confused.

Add to this

If this is all elegy written
every morning but I'm not that
disciplined. Details are lacking.

Emotions and emptiness are lacking.
No philosophy here, no Greek or Latin swerve.
Not even a list of –

Remembering the beginning again
there was something lacking
I didn't want to believe.

All this awaiting revision shifting
laughter and argument across the fence
in a language I haven't begun to understand.

Instead of resolving the problem

Morning outside this sitting
on a grey bench the risk of belief
polyhedral, multi-dimensional
multiply connected that is to say full of holes
a sponge fiction topology foam
what's left of the original hope angle –

Go back to the rain of light.
Church bells. 12:46 p.m. Iambic.

Branches leafed out and flowers even this picture
has no flowers. Also shadows
falling together and the truth of the matter
instead of resolving the problem, give it a name.
Everything will flower at the edge
without finality, no beauty.

Hailing, slant from the north. 12:54 p.m.
Now rain, petals falling, rough constellation.
Sun. 1:02 p.m. 1:13 p.m.

The light that leaks from composition

Thinking the patterns without
patterns not drawing or erasing
every star happened once.

Un-drawing, disordering
possible or pattern radius remains
in the eye and object.

The light that leaks from composition alone
answers this picture with memory or quotation
tedium looking closely discursive even narrative.

Infinite depth of field and radiant geometry
of margins of displacement of the sound
to move through the rooms quickly

enough to find her.

If I am compelled

Illuminated, not another
beyond this faculty of memory desirous
where you can be touched
beyond my own memory how.
If I do not remember.
If I name grief or fear.
If I am compelled to be sad or fearful.
Something needs to be placed here.
Exists outside the event which it constitutes.

Materials

Perhaps there is no truth in.
Perhaps only body in
not to say in senses but piled-up material
words or pages or brush strokes.
One substance cannot be produced by another substance
and subject to passions
but a caress and repeated
without abstraction is memory gentle
an abstraction and does ideal mean?
Forgetfulness also.

The original of

Weighed in difficult dark geometry
rough mass of books or stacked-up dawn
written after its tempting emptiness and small notes.

Revisiting fine lines and perfect eyes.
What colour? Laurel. Original
and occupied black becoming blue or vice versa.

A particular shade of warm or singing I said repeating you
repeating marble or some other metamorphic
trace or swerve sky fire affect in which order is broken.

Solid translation if I tried to doubt everything
of the void that inhabits touch at mourning, without example
knowing numbers attend and search attends.

Singular unneeded light brushing
the rain cliff of breathing dawn shards
and how atoms came later, exultant, jubilant, history –

will have been. This isn't ever about certainty.

If I am completely calm

or not completely
if I move will there be new
constellations or continuing

life. And if I stay
still what life under
this erased hour.

A tree has been projected into the Milky Way.
The word "constellation" is overused.
Stillness promises too much.

An excess

here a surplus a superabundance beyond recognition more
sublime primary emotions or on the other hand appetite
and consciousness thereof just as I remember

myself to have remembered for example groceries
    a dozen brown
that leaves me abstract electric
and not another lifting out or slippery mending illumination

ashes and snapshot streets shiny ink over wash
black after rain the cuffs and collar
of my black suit jacket worn smooth linen

seldom joy beginning or end unqualified
neither an act of memory or gratitude
which opens an abyss and I don't believe you can
    actually recall.

Life. Or, still life.

Bear the words atlas or grey index catalogue golden
exactly two russet apples asymptote bowl rough salt
ellipses down candle ends white string

wrinkled on the table, cinnabar, mercury, green linen
I can't recall which books. Balanced. Porcelain cupping
a pear and a peach loose unlinked lists. Drawing.

No recall. No alchemy. No dark matter. No insurrection.
But ink and five notebooks; later, just two. Black, then red.
Photographs of folded unnecessary thread. Translation

once, a bridge, beginning pages of an essay on desire
everything in this simple and doubled room judged no end
say subject to a mathematical principle –

The world is gone. Those apples have been there
too long. Not everything.
Still life. Or the truth in painting.

Erased

No less than; neither more nor less than, simply.
Taken literally, embodied, an essay.
Not the commonplace of cause. I had no idea.

What will we be for each other you said.
What would the sublime have to do with all
    these inadequations?
I wrote down what you said, definitions.

Not about speaking.
Need became style.
I learned to erase.

If wearing white erased.
If eating erased.
If erased after fast, cold paint the secrets.

We spoke every day.
I sat at your table warm mornings made lists of numbers.
Private keys for public silence.

Not true, erased.

Doubt comes before belief

Without lack of anything
doubt comes before deletion in over
of the heresy we are perfectible belief cloud scars soar.

That low gardens enclose missed voice rose.
That I may not have I.
That my speech my writing is or if.

That the child learns by believing the
kind absence of the goal would not
war in the garden a fire.

When while or well quite late
imagining a final gentle valley landscape sheltered without
photographs a high tower. You tarry. Misheard. Colour.

Measure. Subject. Ash.
That not yet lesson.
A missing line.

And innumerable times again

It will take a while, read slowly
without too much attention
word-shapes, turning pages, the weight of the book
are a comfort and don't construct comfort.
It's easier to read what others have written.
Same-colour stripes on the coffee bowl

when it looks like rain if the forecast doesn't call for it.
Last night the sky was modest with stars.
This spider, this moonlight among the trees, similarly
this moment, and I itself –
There's a cloud that looks like Europe.

I thought I knew

A tree. Of course I'll say an apple tree.
The children climbing and one
too scared to go high. Well then,

you say to them, let's make a painting of it.
I read that and know you at once.
The comfort of bright-apple city lights

imagined stars and the ladder zag of branches.
A crazy-coloured child-bird.
I'm sure you always wanted to wrestle too.

Leaving or arriving

Leaving or arriving anxiety, book by your bed.
Half-packed (or unpacked) suitcase, gooseneck lamp
reading together, and then.

For all the days and nights past
and still to come, you said.
The plural of intensity.

Or is a noun in the construct state
the form it takes when joined
to another noun on which it is dependent.

Someone else writing.

Perhaps touching

Inexact correspondence at least two things
laid beside each other perhaps
touching many things

two bodies perhaps touching separated
only by punctuation
marks not used in my language.

My mouth raw with you remember in a year
will we have remembered
this thirst or just its quenching?

To find the real

I don't write in my books submerge
waking up with the book face-down page folded
my inheritance a cynical optimism or closing my eyes
I have to re-read everything.
Is this a romantic position? In those far places visible shine

discarded objects in the grass, pitted millstones, imagine water,
weathered wood. Black and white. Luminance and chroma
    noise. Old junk.
I am not a modernist *to be stripped of every fiction except one*
the fiction of an absolute early light
with no right to write a word like "angel"–

Thus the angel of electricity.
In the boughs of the tree wolves
toward the top of course.
Apples. Hours. Work.
A polyhedron with at least eight unequal surfaces.

Perhaps I need a solid thing I can turn over and over in
    my hands.

How much past to set aside

in favour of art history
in favour of handwriting and typewriters
in favour of the object letters and post

neither in word
nor meaning

or bark peeled from a tree
remembrance
not to be measured by the parts of time

arranged at random dropped
but soon or eventually the pattern of rain
torn

against which the same sky
unique vanishing point placing
time without qualia the turns

The truth in painting

Clouds evolve, boil, drift there
is no understanding other than painted
landscape is not a narrative
or a window. Is there time
in a painting? Enough
to scrape away colour and emotion perhaps
memory slurring into slides of thick and thin
movement. Misquote or forget.
Not your name. Sky and ground.

Beyond measure

There is time in a landscape it breathes.
Each motion un-held not necessarily
remembered. Danced with to imagine
what we're unable to
doubt comes after.

Not after

In absent wanting by
meadows nor stopping to cut
stalks of indigo asters

the night sky seduced you with
the names of flowers and looked back.
It's all the same deny.

About remember mended light
about all the others.
Enough never until impossible.

Every flower elegy.
Every breath a cloud.
Every real painting.

Watercolour sheets string and brown
wrapping paper secret butcher's paper
stopping life after invisible.

Memory frame

Hung up the key again, sitting, waiting,
roomy comfortable cool.
Cell. Books. Animals. No blame.
Chores to do.
Is it better to write in the kitchen?

Temporality introduces an incurable perfection into the –

What consolation? Philosophy? Love's work?
Without tears folded over and mended
in bright read thread black words border
to give this back to you wanting –

Inspecting nostalgia

1

Told again, thinking this want and have
through odd particular remains, toss and turn
past, taped up, torn out, street lamps throwing dusky half-
lies. End quote. And today I was compelled to walk
the neighbourhood. A man
carrying an umbrella a black umbrella
was coming back from the park
with his dog a black dog.
I walked behind the two
and how the rain made the pavement
blacker. Trees
shielded and revealed the unlit lamps.
In the past the rain was cold.

Today I was tempted to recall
every day the everyday
that I once thought would be.
Laundry in a wicker basket
an iron, a bowl of miso soup.
I determined to list the colours
I remembered when I got home
clothes soaked through by the rain.
I should have been cold.
In the past I would have been cold.

There are good words for this.
I know. I could write them down.
Chimera. Metastable. Sublation. Exposed.
Root. Device. Serene. Westerly.
There's no end to it, to them.

2

I know it's a good question.
Knives and forks in the dishwasher.
There was a river.
Running the icy streets in the dark at the end of the year.

I could make a list. Indexed.
Picture of our first meal. Spoons and plates.
I won't say a picture of our last.
All about preparing food, maybe.

I want to say failure. I want to say gasp.
La mise en abyme. The pluperfect tense. A tension.
Justified. I want to say that was, and yet.

These days I remember three days when
I didn't go outside. Couldn't. Winter, snowing,
and I talked to you on the phone, I think.

3

Yesterday was close to perfect.
I looked at old photographs and read.
I almost sent you a postcard. Stamp-sized.

These streets are mine now. The white cat
I knew as a kitten curls through the fence.

*The suffering caused by an unappeased
yearning to return*? Say more, you said once.
But I like it here. If I'm suffering

it's for more reasons, if that can be.
Sure, this café is the kind of place you'd love.
Even a ghost is like a place. But I can't tell you

without describing how the white cat laps
the milk left for her in a cracked pale saucer,
how she turns, meets my gaze, and walks away.

4

If there are pictures
of the stitching
in the trees.
All repaired flowers.

If always cut.
If always seams.
If always tulips.
If always more

or left the picture rained on
there colour fades, leading to
irreparable.

If that kind of mourning.
Coffee and stitching. Breakfast right.
Not there. Not at all.

5

An avoidance of the avoidance of a word.
Erased love, dust is thick here, but
I really only see it at night.
Dulls presence and absence both.

I don't have a family album.
I don't have photographs
of unnamed uncles in uniform or impossible
young women with baby carriages.

I do have these letters forged in thin
transparent light. An alphabet history.
Some of which actually. I have to say.

Maybe you don't blame me after all.
Only get to solid black and real
after giving up this ghost of colour.

6

Quote beauty is no veil,
destroys with
the loyalty of a habit.
Wasted intensity!

Read too much.
Not enough out loud
nor to you now
voiceless stars.

Want to be interrupted.
Night order of listening and lack
broken by a flashbulb.
Exposed anxious ghosts

found wanting. Found out.
Found wanting in.

7

Its nature fragments by its nature
endless and ending. That means
tomorrow I might wake up
in a hotel which is nothing like
where I met you. The café
full of dancers drinking Evian.
I'm wasting my time here.
We're all wasting our time here.

That shame diagnosis: lost time,
a misplaced ring to it, a wan interval
all proven ineffectual – can never be, is always
more. Nothing other than that loss and the desire
it dances with maybe spends the night.

At this table with a glass of water.
Ring between my thumb and forefinger
tapping it on the tabletop.
The sparkling stainless-steel click
of repeated desire locking into place.
A solid memory waking up
then falling apart always in plain view.

Afterword and critique

I

The transient catch the best catch
I can at impossible permanent.
Porcelain light full of dust.
Dust marking the visible real edge catch.
Broken pieces of seeing and remembering dust
and feeling clot a ruined field of view.

II

Those rusted bicycle frames you see locked
up, no wheels, no seat, chain drooping?

Did you promise something? Did I?

III

Even giving up I think of myself
younger and taller than I am.
Secured. More whole. Disappointed.
I know it isn't there, but
I can't find it just now.

IV

Affect can't be system.
Or coloured in. Or dusted, like graffiti.
Nothing extra. Ordinary
lyric repair: a memory wound,
a piercing, a decoration –
the catalogue of and other
late-night reading.

V

It made sense.

Lambswool. Sprockets. Labelled drawers of pills and bottle caps. The boarded-up consulate. Neptune. The devil. Portobello Road. Shade. Stars. A colander. Brake pads. A watch battery. (Does anyone mend pots anymore?) Nitroglycerin. Low light. Low life. Low pressure. Black. Crane. Ginger. A jar of cold cream. A jar of leftover satellite. A jar of blue tire scraps. A parabola, still. An entire life of Princess Marie von Thurn und Taxis-Hohenlohe. A can opener. An Allen wrench. An apple. A pretense. Slipping into the dictionary like a curious dog, or my other ice. Predictable constellation. Less.

Knew.

Sources

No language stands alone. My writing is made of scraps and fragments picked up here and there. Some are mine and some aren't; some of the sources of the words in this book are listed here. I try to keep track but I do miss things, for which I apologize. Thanks to all the writers from whom I've borrowed and from whom I've learned.

The epigraphs are from "And *Ut Pictura Poesis* Is Her Name" by John Ashbery and "The Composition of the Cell" by Lyn Hejinian.

The phrase "Time is lyric's dark counterpoise" is from Jan Zwicky's *Lyric Philosophy.*

The phrase "a clock in the shape of a heart" is from "A man who snatches a ring" by Anna Mendelssohn.

"Diamonds Are a Girl's Best Friend" is a song from the musical *Gentlemen Prefer Blondes* and was written by Jule Styne and Leo Robin.

"She didn't learn to tell time until her mid-teens" was said of Emily Dickinson by someone on the Internet. I don't believe it.

The phrase "In the rain, as if there were no need for a taxi to take us away" is from a letter written on July 16, 1958, by Ingeborg Bachmann to Paul Celan, translated from the German by Wieland Hoban.

The phrase "The divergence between enjoying and knowing," which is used as the title of a poem in an earlier section, is also from this essay.

The phrase "I will think of you in my other poems" is from "Earrings Dangling and Miles of Desert" by Gary Snyder.

"The Truth in Painting" is the title of a book by Jacques Derrida, translated from the French by Geoff Bennington and Ian McLeod. Many of the poems in this section quote fragmentary phrases from the essay "Parergon" in this book, as well as Kant's *Critique of Judgment*, which is the subject of that essay.

The phrase "The light that leaks from composition alone" is from *Melencholia* by Clark Coolidge.

The phrase "doubt comes before belief" is misquoted from section 160 of Ludwig Wittgenstein's *On Certainty*, translated from the German by G.E.M Anscombe and G.H. von Wright. The quotation from Wittgenstein's *Tractatus Logico-Philosophicus*, translated from the German by D.F. Pears and B.F. McGuinness, used as the title of a poem, is not misquoted.

The phrase "this spider, this moonlight among the trees, similarly this moment" is from Friedrich Nietzsche's *The Gay Science*, translated from the German by Josefine Nauckhoff and modified slightly.

The poems "I thought I knew" and "Leaving or arriving" have their origins in two paintings by Charlotte Salomon, one of which is part of her "play with music," *Life? Or Theatre?*

"To be stripped of every fiction except one / the fiction of an absolute" are lines from "Notes toward a Supreme Fiction" by Wallace Stevens.

The phrase "temporality introduces an incurable perfection into the very essence of the present" is from Proust, in *Jean Santeuil,* translated from the French by Roger Shattuck in his book *Proust's Way.*

"The suffering caused by an unappeased yearning to return" is the definition of nostalgia given by Milan Kundera in his novel *Ignorance,* translated from the French by Linda Asher.

Fragments of text also come (some through the work of various unacknowledged translators) from Saint Augustine, Francis Bacon, Ted Berrigan, Anne Carson, Raymond Chandler, Emily Dickinson, Eihei Dōgen, Elsa Dorfman, Friedrich Hölderlin, Hugh Hood, Julian of Norwich, Jean-François Lyotard, Vladimir Nabokov, Chantal Neveu, George Oppen, Erwin Panofsky, Anna Pavord, Marjorie Perloff, Rainer Maria Rilke, W.G. Sebald, Baruch Spinoza, Wikipedia, the anonymous authors of email spam and website comments, and others I've no doubt forgotten.

Acknowledgments

Some of these poems previously appeared in slightly different forms in *ditch, E·ratio, The Puritan,* and *(parenthetical)*. Thanks to the editors.

At different times and in different places, in 2010 and 2011, Jay MillAr, Erín Moure, and Alice Notley facilitated workshops in the context of which some of these poems were written, revised, or conceived. Thanks to them, and to everyone who participated, for their thoughts and attentive reading.

Sachiko Murakami, my editor for this book, helped smooth out the rough edges, file away the burrs, and burn the rejects. Thanks, Sachi: without you, every other word in this book might have been "still." You are awesome!

Finally, the poem that begins this book, "Before," is for Eva-Marie Stern, because she liked it so much when she read it back in 2004.

About the author

R. Kolewe lives in Toronto. *Inspecting Nostalgia* is his second collection of poems. His first, *Afterletters*, was published by BookThug in 2014.